Toes, Toads, Tulips & Turtles

A Miscellany of Verse

Mike Orlock

FOUR WINDOWS PRESS | STURGEON BAY, WISCONSIN

Copyright © 2021 by **Mike Orlock**

All rights reserved. No part of this publication may be reproduced, distributed, or transmitted in any form or by any means, without prior written permission.

Mike Orlock and Four Windows Press
231 N Hudson Ave.
Sturgeon Bay, WI 54235
 www.fourwindowspress1.com

Publisher's Note: This is a work of poetry. Names, characters, places, and incidents are a product of the author's imagination. Locales and public names are sometimes used for poetic purposes. Any resemblance to actual people, living or dead, or to businesses, companies, events, institutions, or locales is completely coincidental.

Book Layout © 2017 BookDesignTemplates.com

Toes, Toads, Tulips & Turtles. — 1st ed.

ISBN: 978-0-9991957-4-1

Acknowledgments

The following selections first appeared on *Your Daily Poem* website in 2022: "Considering the Common Wren," "Keeping Time," "Under a Sturgeon Moon," and "Word Walking."

The following selections originally appeared in *Moss Piglet* (info@krazines.com) in 2022: "Dung Beetle Medley," "Ode to an Ugly Toad," and "Stranger in a Strange Poem."

"The Adulting of Rebecca Kleefish" originally appeared in the pages of *The Peninsula Pulse,* Door County, Wisconsin.

I must also acknowledge the generous support, tireless effort, and extreme patience of Tom Davis of Four Windows Press, without whom this book would not exist.

COVER DESIGN AND DRAWING BY RORI ORLOCK

Table of Contents

I — 10

Write Me a Poem — 11
How to Dream a (Door County) Poem: — 12
March Mania — 13
Life's a (Lacuna*) Beach — 14
The Thing About Hair — 15
Toe Ditty — 17
Considering the Common Wren — 19
Gulper Eels Exegesis — 20
Ruminations on an Earwig — 21
Ode to the Mosquito — 22
To a Worm, Waiting Its Turn — 23
Ode to an Ugly Toad — 25
Tick Time Too — 27
In Tribute to the Trusty Testudine — 28
My Penultimate Tomato — 29
Petrichor — 31
The Night Storm — 32
Perpetual Winter Comes a'Calling — 33
A World Without Words, Amen — 35
Dung Beetle Medley — 36
Note to a Tulip — 38
Cirrus Circus Calliope — 40
A Small Poem About a Thing Significant — 41

Under a Sturgeon Moon _____ 42

2 _____ 43

First Thirsts _____ 44
Condimentia _____ 46
Old Saw Singing _____ 47
The Effete Charms of Modern Poesy _____ 48
Word Walking _____ 49
Couch-Boat: A Memory _____ 51
The Reunion _____ 53
Let's Go, Door County! _____ 55
Drift _____ 57
Stranger in a Strange Poem _____ 59
Wedding Homily, for Nick and Amanda _____ 61
Wordsmithing _____ 62
Keeping Time _____ 64
The Years of Living Vicariously _____ 65
Running On Beyond _____ 67
Playing Dead _____ 68
"Kapricious" _____ 69
Speaking Haiku to 17 Fifth graders _____ 71
It Ain't the Money, Honey _____ 73
Senior Surprises _____ 76
My Life in Pink _____ 78
Tiresias Untuned _____ 79
The Opposite of Sex _____ 81

Forensic Analysis _____ 83

3 _____ **85**

What a Poem Can Do _____ 86
The Misuse of Silence _____ 87
Eating Our Own _____ 88
Patience and the Pain of Becoming _____ 90
Grief _____ 92
Reductive Reasoning _____ 94
Prepositions of Grief _____ 95
Sleep, a Lullaby _____ 97
Assignment _____ 98
John _____ 100
About Bill _____ 102
Bedouins _____ 104
Being Betty _____ 107

4 _____ **109**

If William Carlos Williams Lived My Life _____ 110
Trippy _____ 111
Stopping by Daffodils on a Chilly Evening, or _____ 112
Thirteen Ways of Looking at a Gun _____ 114

5 _____ **117**

Earth Day Elegy, 2022 _____ 118

Upon Reading the Marshall Islands Are Sinking _____120
Eight Top Species Threatened by Climate Change ___122
A Poem for My Conservative Friends_____123
Moving Closer to a Distant Reality _____125
The Dead of War Speak Their Piece in Silence _____126
Deconstructing Kyle Rittenhouse _____127
The Perks of Burning Books in South Dakota _____128
Supremely Courted, a Judicious Review _____129
The Adulting of Rebecca Kleefisch_____131
Trump's Big Lie_____132
Lost in Grammarica _____134

6 _____**135**

Expressing (Trains in Four Tracks)_____136
Old Goat, Scrounging _____138
(A Self-Assessment of Sorts) _____138
Satisfying Conclusions _____139
Practical(ly) Poetry _____140
Word Wastrel: A Life Devised in Four Stanzas_____142
About the Author_____145

I

Write Me a Poem

I like a poem to bend in ways
that don't quite break, that take
turns I can't anticipate like a coaster
rolling with reckless speed
over-under-sideways-down
until finally easing to a stop
that leaves me breathless to read it
again. I want a poem to ride
me as I wrangle it, buck back hard
with a spirit that defies reason, dares me
to consume it in sloppy swallows
that fill me to bursting
until I am hollow for more.

Give me a poem like that,
one that gets so far under my skin
it becomes like blood and bone,
one I feel with every step,
bouncing on the feet of its meter.
Write me a poem that splatters me with syntax,
then washes me clean in the spill of its thrill
of being so alive with words it knows
it will sweeten someone's tongue tomorrow.
Write me that kind of poem today,
one that never acts its age, but stays instead
forever young on tiptoe.

How to Dream a (Door County) Poem:

Lay back, close your eyes.

Crack an idea into a blue bowl of sky
under a sun especially high
on a day so much like another
you couldn't distinguish one from the other.
Fold in words of no particular importance
except they matter to you in that moment.
Stir into stanzas and whip to a whimsy
in tropes of clouds parading as poesy.

If your poem aspires to meaning and merit,
beat down notions of wisdom and wit
(with a cool beverage if one is handy)
until your concoction approximates candy.
When assonance and consonance reach prodigality,
edit out logic with utmost frugality.
Then let this mess within your mind sit
until something miraculous seems to come of it.

Tuck it away for a day you really need it.

March Mania

I feel a poem coming on.
This time of year here in Wisconsin,
February gray begrudgingly gives way
to March brown as patches of ground
emerge from under cover of white
on days the sun seems blindingly bright;

I sense a stirring of nouns begin to take root
under foot, a vagary of verbs in pursuit
of a moment, gerunds festering to foment,
as an irruption of phrases dazzles and dazes
a landscape transformed from barren cold
to brazen bold reborn in torrents of spring;

I divine bolts of birds suddenly heard
again, strung like prepositions across the sky,
connecting morning to afternoon and evening
in lines that lift my own spirit to fly full
into the face of things, washing winter
from my eyes with the first rains of rhyme.

Life's a (Lacuna*) Beach

*(*noun*) an unfilled space or missing portion in a manuscript

If life is a poem,
one we're constantly composing,
arranging words in witty ways
that squeeze meaning from our musing,
searching for a rhythm
without tripping over feet
while teasing out the tangles
of metaphor in rhymes discrete,
then those gaps between the stanzas,

the ones that carry us in leaps
of time and space in memory
over a broken stretch of beach,
eliding from a past tense
to a future perfect distant
of all we will have been doing
in what seems a lifelong instant,

shouldn't all those holes we've filled
in the act of our revising,
that hide the empty hours
of our wasted temporizing,
inform the very substance of the text
that we are living,
all those precious minutes squandered
in the service of self-giving?

If my life is truly poetry,
I sense its meaning is abstruse:
Mine's not lyric, epic or ballad
but haiku—one quite obtuse.

The Thing About Hair

Funny how a head of hair
full and flowing down to there
or there!
        or there!
                or there!
                      or there!
can conjure romance in the air
can make a man more debonair
or lend a woman *savoir faire*
in social situations where
a toss of curls adds such flair
in the flush of flirting, *c'est la guerre*.

Thick and lustrous, gorgeous locks!
Fetishized and prized, in shocks
loose or clipped, bobbed or boxed,
braided, brushed-back, girly, goth,
slicked or shaved, tinted or topped,
hair is what the world takes stock
of whom we are and how we rock
to part ourselves from the flock.

How strange, then, that a single hair,
separate from the head it shares
and all the other hair grown there,
found floating in a soup somewhere,
or there!
        or there!
                or there!
                      or there!
(it doesn't matter much what fare)

will gag our appetite, laid bare,
disgusted by one errant hair.

That's the hairy thing in matters most hirsute:
We adore the luscious lot, abhor the wayward shoot.

Toe Ditty

I remember a time my toes were young,
young and fashionably free—
of socks, of shoes,
of the social shackles
that determined how toes should be seen.

Boy toes and girl toes were just toes,
after all. They came five to a foot,
totaling ten; but big toe to piggy
they walked separate paths
into lives that defined what we'd be.

Boy toes were taught to toe lines,
toe marks, dig in, ignore getting stubbed.
They might bend, even break,
but keeping on them each day
gave boys the chance to be men.

Girl toes were supposed to twinkle
and dance, in polishes pink and red.
They were meant to peek
from the tips of some shoes
or from under the hem of a dress.

Girl toes were prized for their shape
and their size—as girls were, too,
more or less. Boy toes could be
rough and thick as a tree, as long
as they climbed with each step.

These days my toes look old as I feel—
knobby, gnarly and bent.

18 · TOADS, TOES, AND TULIPS

When they tingle or ache
it's not from merriment's sake,
but the cold, the years that I've spent

standing on tiptoe, vying and trying,
straining to seem somewhat taller.
Now buckled at knuckles,
they curl inside socks,
making my feet that much smaller.

Considering the Common Wren

Everything a wren is
is evident in the twitch
of tail feathers, head, and wings
that indicate an itch
to change a peak perspective
to hop from perch to perch
to zero/zoom on some small thing
within aspect of its search.

For that essential something
that something that it wants
is coiled in its bearing
compelling it to hunt;
if not behind this leaf or twig
that bush or bark or bough
if not somewhere on this tree
to another it will go.

How like me most mornings
pecking through my words
alert to find the finest ones
the choicest nouns and verbs
to fill an empty appetite
for a fulsome phrase or line;
like my friend, the common wren
I'm searching all the time.

Gulper Eels Exegesis

from a watercolor by Peggy Macnamara

Is under water like outer space,
a place no one can hear a scream?
Do those poor creatures your diet features
utter surprise or cry their pain
when the needle teeth in your cavernous mouth
(large as a crypt and just as dark)
bite into pulp without hesitation,
before you swallow without mastication,
consuming them whole in a single gulp?

You, pelican of the darkest deep,
you glide, you swerve, you dive, you curve
your sinuous body just a glimpse
of what this world truly portends
for any living thing seduced by the beauty of your glow:
Death comes from above or below
in a moment's merciless measure,
and what we believe of ourselves in God's plan
is some other thing's devilish pleasure.

Ruminations on an Earwig

I wonder what who made you had in mind,
the way you've been conceived of and designed.
You seem bizarrely backwards, ill-defined:
Those fearsome pincers that you drag behind,
are they for show or something to remind
us that the world is sometimes less than kind?

You seem to favor shadows, damp and dark.
I found you in the mulch, under the bark,
your body black and brilliant as a spark,
wriggling escape from light without remark.
Is life for you, like me, an abstruse arc
of moments lush and lovely, cold, and stark?

I suppose you might see me as I see you,
a curiosity that's strangely new.
We are, from now, conjoined in what we do,
with scripted parts to play without purview.
—Does a God of earwigs cherish or eschew
His frightened children when their bit is through?

Ode to the Mosquito

O, little fly whose slight, vampirish sting
can cause the end of life with just one bite;
you are the master in each dank domain
you thrive and hide yourself in open sight.
No woods or jungle, fields or fetid plain
is free of your pernicious influence;
you swarm in numbers beyond imagining
and revel in your deadly pestilence.
There is no living thing you cannot kill,
and mortal man knows well to fear your drone;
you leave your mark in welts that itch and swell,
and though your life is short, the strife is long.
O, doyenne of disease, mistress of floods—
what made you mocks belief in loving gods.

To a Worm, Waiting Its Turn

I imagine you underfoot,
underground near some root, sensing me
pushing a mower back and forth
receding lines of chemically enhanced lawn
in mindless repetition, as you turn,
mindfully tunneling through a blackness
beyond my comprehension,
recycling refuse into the rich earth
from which grass is seasonally reborn.

I know you have no eyes with which to see,
no ears with which to hear,
no nose with which to smell the world, unlike me—
your existence locked inside a body
that doesn't require the attention
and obsession that I daily devote my own.
I envy you that:
Both male and female simultaneously one,
reproducing yourself double the sum,
you are free from the s/expectations
we as a species have religiously imposed upon ourselves
to be men and women at our best
(even if we act like worms at our worst).

We humans like to think
we've got this evolution business licked:
If life is a pyramid scheme, we're at the point;
you're somewhere near rock bottom.
Yet you seem to persevere despite everything
we dish out, waiting while we kill ourselves
with carbohydrates and cholesterol,
plastics and polyfluorinates. In our arrogance

we celebrate ourselves for consuming the planet
in bits, one bite at a time, willfully
blind to what we soon will be—
the feast upon which your kind dine.

Ode to an Ugly Toad

Common Surinam toad named Amazon Rain Forest's ugliest creature.
                                                     Quora Digest

If ugly is in the eye,
then beauty must be buried
somewhere deep within
your blistered skin,
Princess *Pipa Pipa* of the Amazon,
stargazer from Surinam.

(A Trypophobe's nightmare)

you are cursed with carrying your young
fully formed in numbers tenfold ten
for weeks and weeks on end,
until they burst from boils on your back,
a honeycombed eruption of life,
baby toads upon baby toads tumbling,

(in a Darwinian's dream)

slithering through the ooze
of amniotic love to life. They leave you
all at once without return,
without cursory concern,
to embark upon their own
journey in joyful pursuit

(of a mother's imperative):

*Find your place in paradise
born where you belong,*

*in beauty beheld within
our verdant jungle home,
to begin again once again
your life, this poem.*

Tick Time Too

A hot match for you seems the skin on my back
and that cruel little mouth of yours
that digs in to feed so impolitely.
You invite yourself to feast among my freckles,
pretending in your deception to be one,
but that bulging body of yours becomes too unsightly
to ignore. Deer and dogs aren't enough for you:
You want more. And when you've had your fill,
like other blood suckers of your ilk,
you leave behind a soupcon of corruption,
just a little evil something to remember you by.

You pack more misery than can be imagined
into that bit of a body you inhabit;
it's tempting to think you man-made, not divine.
But if God made man in his musings,
He must have made you too,
as just a trick to pique His devilish side—
give us His chosen children another torment to survive.

In Tribute to the Trusty Testudine

O, to be so immutable!
With an outward expression *that* inscrutable!
Taking with you accommodations movable,
your entire existence quite behoovable:
Vulnerable extremities fully retractable,
house and home efficiently compactable.
You are a marvel among things ontological
looking to adapt to changes ecological!

Tortoise or terrapin, loggerhead, or box,
leatherback or painted, hawksbill or musk,
you come in an assortment of sizes and bulk,
from midget to mammoth, dainty to hulk;
you move at a pace best described as a poke
(unless in the water, where you glide with each stroke)
and though you've been taunted by fleet-footed hares,
you outlive them by decades, outpace them by years.

You rest where you stand, impervious to time,
in construction and character, a flawless design.
Your legacy can trace to the dinosaurs of yore,
but your lineage remains while theirs is no more.
Your descendants ascendant despite every storm
as species around you die off with alarm.
Man likes to fancy himself in God's image,
but what if our Maker has a testudinal visage?

My Penultimate Tomato

I can't remember my first tomato
(who remembers a first tomato?)
and I don't want to remember my last,
because—you know—it will *be* the last;
but I want to remember in all its ripeness,
its tang-on-the-tongue bursting sweetness
that next-to-last tomato to grace
a salad or sauce I'll ever taste
before such a thing as tomatoes
matter to me no more.

Call me the sentimental type.
I've developed quite a crush on living
in this world, despite the difficulties
of finding a reliable plumber
on a holiday weekend or making a left
turn against traffic during rush hour.
I figure since I've come this far,
nearly three quarters of the way in,
I want to hang around long as I can
just to see what happens next.

So I've taken to watching people more
and the news less. I've started listening
to voices on the street and in stores
instead of the noise that engulfs me
daily. And I watch with fascination
the choices people make, especially
when it comes to tomatoes in the grocery.
Why that particular one, why that variety?
What drives us to choose the things we do
one moment to the next?

I concentrate now on the taste and texture
of every tomato I buy and slice, boil or bake,
figuring this one might be the penultimate
to bring the dish I'm preparing
that distinctive tomato flavor. As long as I can
remember *this* one, I say to myself,
there will always be one more tomorrow
that I'll get to savor again. It's a game
I play with myself, and with every next tomato
I win.

Petrichor

NOUN: A distinctive scent, usually described as earthy, pleasant, or sweet, produced by rainfall on very dry ground.

It's the brand of perfume
Earth wears,
a beguiling intoxicant
for all who have flowered
and flourished within
the enchantment
of her summer scent.

It's the world's fragrance
we inhale lastly,
life's essence
we cling to fastly, for
each borrowed breath
is an encumbrance,
our passing recompense.

The Night Storm

It creeps upon us under cover of darkness,
a presence forming on the sleep side of thinking
when seeming and dreaming are one and the same;
until that rumbling tumble of throat-clearing thunder,
once so distant it was a mumble in the mind,
suddenly blows through the open window
with a breath redolent of ozone and rain.

What follows the first fat drops is a drumming
beating a rhythm on the rooftop and panes,
and the scene outside, defined in bright flashes,
surrenders itself to the pummeling wind.
It's then when the storm makes clear the connection
between us and the world in the immense sweep of time:
We are a murmur, a flicker of lightning, no more lasting
than the brief storm outside.

Perpetual Winter Comes a'Calling

Winter blew into town
mid-November last year
just before Thanksgiving,
got comfortable and settled in
like a relative you don't mind
seeing around the holidays
as long as you know
he doesn't intend to stay;
but this Winter had
what you'd say are
"other ideas."

Come February, we all thought
winter might want to take
a little break, see
a bit of the country
he hasn't visited in a while,
clap some backs
and chap some hands
of other folks he knows;
but this winter
wouldn't go with the flow.
He doubled down.

By March, we were all
dropping hints, grumbling
that winter had
outstayed his welcome;
maybe it was time for him
to pack it in,
head back north—
See you again next year;

but this winter said
with perpetual sincerity,
"I like it here!"

Seems he has a thing
for April, a month that can
melt the iciest heart when she
wants, but who can be
every bit the bitch T. S. Eliot
said she was when she gets
in one of her tempers.
Perpetual winter seems smitten;
tells us, "Don't put away
those scarves and mittens yet,
folks. I'm thinking I might stay."

A World Without Words, Amen

Another workshop.
Another prompt:

> *Nature…*
> *Landscapes…*
> *Sunlight…*
> *Spring…*

Get out there and let the beauty of the season move you to write…

Shit.
I left the words for this poem back at the workshop,
on the table next to my smart phone.

I'm stuck with what the trees give me:

Similes fall like seeds in the breeze,
and metaphors blink in a budding of leaves,
inviting me to contemplate the meaning of a cardinal calling
to seduce a mate, its pickup line repeated to refrain.

The morning ripens round me
into sun-soaked spring, and I think,
This is going to be a really nice day!
but the flowers already know that
without benefit of a weather app.

Unlike me, bees don't need a clock to tell time,
just as birds don't need words
to make a rhyme…

or prompt a poem.

Dung Beetle Medley

There's so much shit in this world,
it's a wonder we can work it out.
Us, up to our necks in it daily;
you, moving mountains of it nightly.
The two of us needing raincoats, really,
rolling in it,
tunneling through it,
dwelling under it.

You've got no time to waste
working eight days a week.
Every night's a hard day's night
when your inside's out and your outside's in
deep shit so heavy it's driving you mad.

You flew in the face of Zeus
on Mount Olympus, no less,
you crazy little dung-dozer,
just to prove a point:
You might eat shit to live
but that doesn't mean you have to take it.
Jai guru deva, om, your ass.
Nothing's going to change your world
without you giving two shits about it.

Eagles might rule the sky,
shitting on you every chance they get,
but only *you* can roll the sun across the heavens,
King Tut believed, and that's some *serious* shit
to hold to, or savor, as the case may be.

So, keep those joo joo eyeballs open
and your shit wired tight.
Four thousand holes in Blackburn Lancashire
need filling, and that shit will take all night.
But, *shit*—that's your thing, right?

Note to a Tulip

Silly, this,
dropping a note to a flower
disguised as a poem.
You can get away with things
in a poem you'd get looked at sideways
writing anything else.
(Try writing an office memorandum
to a chrysanthemum;
you'll get your ass fired,
but quick! *I know*.)

A poem, though,
cuts you some slack.
Makes you look like the sensitive type,
arty and erudite.
Address it to a flower,
everyone's got your back.
Shows you've got
aesthetics out the yin yang
(which happens to be a flower, too,
for those of you doubting
my devotion to botany,
especially to one particular
herbaceous bulbiferous geophyte
growing in a garden down the block).

That's you, royal red Triumph.
I watched you burst from a bulb
mid-April, just a slender green shoot
skinny as a toothpick poking
through the mulch. Two weeks
later, you were knee high and thick

as a stick, standing half a foot
taller than the daffodils
that crowded round you.
Your ruby head bobbing
in the slightest breeze,
you always seemed as interested
in me walking by with my dog
as I was you.

Anyway, my little *lilieae*,
you've made my spirits soar these days
of post-pandemic anticipation
just by being that harbinger of Spring
I've been waiting for so long. Only now
that your flower has fully bloomed,
your mornings greeting me are numbered
as your petals. Our time together is
fleeting, on loan. (Go ahead and groan,
but I've got to make this thing
sound like a legitimate poem, otherwise
I'll find myself planted in a home somewhere
and next May you'll be wondering,
What the hell happened
to that crazy old man and his dog?)

Until next year, my perennial friend,
thanks for hanging around
and enduring the indignities
imposed upon you by my uncouth hound,
whose appreciation of flowers seems
limited to sniffing out and christening
newfound ground. Yours,

Cirrus Circus Calliope

There up above us
higher than stratus
lighter than cumulus
whiter than nimbus
a circus of cirrus
so high and imperious
a calliope of clouds
for the cirrus-curious:

Cirrus *fibratus*
Cirrus *uncinus*
Cirrus *spissatus*
Cirrus *castellanus*
Cirrus *floccus*
Cirrus *intortus*
Cirrus *vertebratus*
Cirrus *radiatus*...

So much cirrus, seriously,
I'm cirrus*ly* delirious.
This poem has become
in substance and sum
a cirrus cloud thesaurus!

A Small Poem About a Thing Significant

So much of man's ambition,
so much his heart's affinity,
so much his soul's volition,
blessed by serendipity;

so much his self-assurance,
so much of what he builds,
so much his fierce persistence
to summit every hill;

so much his carnal passions,
so much his appetites,
so much the things he fashions
forged for what he fights;

so much his grand achievements,
so much his life-long labor,
so much his day's contentment
depends on toilet paper.

Under a Sturgeon Moon

August nights can be sweltering affairs.
Summer heat this time of year
can stew, stagnant and stale, dank
as the vegetables grown ripe too early
in gardens that once seemed lively and lush,
now listless and lank in the sultry air.

The month has the feel of compromise
and yield, as we mark time in a steady march
to the inevitable surrender of fall.
But that moon!
Bright as a bauble
dangling from a necklace of stars,
it hangs overhead like a trophy sturgeon
in the cool depths of sky, awaiting its waning
in glorious gold, igniting dreams once more
of life treasured, of bounty restored.

2

First Thirsts

We kissed before we knew what we were
sealing, for the first time outside a party
after work. You made me wait
while you, inside, were changing
from what you wore to waitress
to what you'd wear that night.

I stood in shadows sipping from two cans,
both foaming over, the beer a metaphor
of what I felt within, while rock 'n roll
reverberated through open windows
and a steady stream of people came and went.
Then you appeared so suddenly before me,
in a dress of hibiscus blooms swirling
in dim porch light. I stood there like a fool,
struck silent—until your smile
brought me back to life.

You slid between my arms and, in your advantage,
held my face to yours with hands so warm,
while I embraced you awkwardly with my elbows,
my hands held wide, beer dripping on the lawn.

Your lips were moist and tangy with fresh gloss,
something citrusy that lingered on my tongue,
while yours surprised me, sneaking into my mouth
to flirt before retreating to your own.

As kisses go, this one wasn't epic, nothing
like in a movie where passions spark to flame.
What did we know of marriage,
children, mortgages, and investment?

We were ourselves just kids:
all we knew was what we wanted
and all we wanted was what we later did.

Yet this first brief spontaneous locking of our lips,
this unexpected awkward clumsy kiss,
stirred within me something elemental—
a thirst for you, so fiercely fundamental,
a taste of what we'd be, sweetly incremental,
I like to think that we were born from this.

Condimentia

My wife is condimentally challenged.
Who else but she
(and others equally of her ilk)
would think it proper
to squeeze ketchup on a hot dog?

Mustard—yes; relish—certainly.
Even horseradish if one desires
(a walk on the wild side of propriety)
dressing one's dog for a robust
romp among the tastier buds.

But ketchup is a cardinal sin
in the culinary catechism of meats
(salted, processed, and packaged)
handed down to us by our forefathers,
whose strict dietary canon commands:

If thy sandwich meat be long and thin,
keep ketchup in yon icebox bin.
Save the savory sauce of the tomato
for your burgers and, perhaps, potato.
But never dress a dog in red,
lest people pity what's in thine head.

I tell my wife there are sumptuary laws
one should never tamper with
(at risk of being ridiculed)
and the rules of condiments are fixed.
"Bite me," she responds.

Proving some tongues are impervious to taste,
no matter how much food for thought is mustered.

Old Saw Singing

Now the nights are longer
I spend my daylight savings thinking
thoughts the kind old men
do drinking: How much more
of what I had is left for me to have?
How little less there seems to be
when sunset drains the glass
to dregs, and old saws do the singing.

Their song is like the finest whine:
It cuts through all the bleating.
A saw unseen but handy still,
despite the years and use,
will bite into what time remains
to keep itself kept—
welcoming one last ruse
to sing what would be wept.

The Effete Charms of Modern Poesy

I watch them through the window of my laptop,
decked out in fancy duds of arty design
teetering from line to line on high heels
of preposterous pretense, so pleased—

they're grand with the courtly come-on,
know all the right runes
to reel a rube like me in; they
make me dream stars instead of stones

as they polish syntax into tiaras
and dab trope behind their ears and knees,
just enough to give a whiff of want
when they brush up against my ambition; these

glitterati of the literati circle set sashaying—
O, how I've lusted to have one mine
for just a moment or two, those
sirens of glossy pages and *New Yorker* sophistication!

Knowing as I do my own grave limitations,
I'm not the tuxedo type, me;
send me out with one of them as arm candy,
I'll trip over my own cosmopolitan desires,

face plant in the gutter
quicker than I can step up to promenade.
Taste them stones, see them stars, all right—
some Windows are just meant for dazing.

Word Walking

I soddle
and doddle,
I nuddle
and scunge;
I dander
and meander,
I wander
and lunge;

I ramble
and shamble,
I saunter
and trip;
I hobble
and toddle,
I mosey
and skip;

I clump
and I stump,
I troop
and I traipse;
I swagger
and stagger,
I pound
and I pace;

I leave there
to get here,
and once here
I'm there;
my life is

a long walk
shuffling
somewhere.

Couch-Boat: *A Memory*

Of course, the couch in Nana and Papa's basement
wasn't a boat, but we made it one those Sundays
we would gather there for supper after church.
Our mothers would cluster in the kitchen,
our fathers around the Zenith color console
in the living room, and we would scurry down
the stairs into the basement where an old brown sofa
sat against a far wall, begging us to make it feel useful
again, if only for an afternoon.

It had been moved there sometime past.
Its four cushions, material worn threadbare
and stained by years of use, stretched
between bulbous armrests inlaid with wood
that looked like the bulwarks of a ship.
The far-left quarter was designed to recline,
and a handle on that side was perfect for re-purposing
as a rudder, so we made this couch
our lifeboat, adrift on a sea of cement, surviving
the storms of our imagination in endless variations
of a game we named Boat.

The eight of us, cousins from three families,
four girls and four boys in ages that spanned a handful
of years, ignored the ambient adult sounds
filtering down from upstairs—the footfalls
from the kitchen and dining room, the chatter
and laughter from the living room—so wrapped were we
in the various scenarios we improvised for ourselves
in our play. Someone was always falling overboard
and hanging on for dear life. We boys might morph
quite suddenly into sharks, thrashing in the water

and terrorizing the girls, who clung to each other,
screaming and laughing. The boat tossed and rolled
across an ocean of frenetic playacting until—

quite suddenly, a door would open,
a shaft of light would illuminate the stairway
like sun from between storm clouds,
and a voice would call us to dinner.
All the drama we were involved in surviving
would resolve itself in an instant.
We'd race each other up the stairs, leaving
that old, battered couch anchored against the wall,
rocking in our wake, awaiting our return.

The Reunion

For the California Cousins: Debbie, Terrie Sue, Tina, Jeralyn, Henry & Mark

It must be mental-muscle-memory:
You haven't seen these people in years,
since a time too distant to clearly remember,
but you can pick them out from across a crowded room
without any difficulty at all.
The decades drop away from faces
to reveal what you knew them to be
back when skin was smooth, eyes
were bright, and bodies could bend
in ways impossible now to comprehend.

First cousins on your mother's side,
from an era when children were born
in multiples, you were mere weeks
(or maybe a few months) apart in age,
and you knew each other in ways
that made you more than close friends.
Those times when families gather
brought you together at holidays,
birthdays, graduations, weddings, even funerals.
You would fall into easy conversation or play,
locked in a moment so self-contained
it seemed those hours would fold
into themselves so that time itself
was a loop, endlessly replayed.

Then life happened.
You went to school, moved away;
met friends, made work,
married, and somewhere in the midst of all that living

you lost touch with each other.
Time became chronological,
and "family" became a parade of names
marching past in Facebook posts.
You kept "in touch" less than colleagues
and acquaintances do, any news of note
condensed in Christmas card greetings
or the odd bit of gossip conveyed
through grapevines, family or otherwise.
We became those adults in the rooms upstairs,
above the basements of the houses
where once we entertained ourselves for hours
in self-scripted games of "horses" and "boat,"
so vividly imagined, a cold cement floor
could transform from rolling hills to raging ocean
in an instant just by saying so.

Now we talk through this reunion
as our grandchildren play silly games
that consume them, and just for today
we glimpse what we were in their faces
and hear what we sounded like when we were kids
and had each other to hold to against
all that growing up we'd be forced to do.
We hug, we joke, we laugh, we tell, we try
to get a half century into a few lines—
and we lie, knowing this might be it
despite promises and resolutions
"to do this again soon," because, as we've learned,
that's the way the world works:
"Ready or not, here it comes!"

But this one afternoon it comes when we're ready,
and like the children we once were,
we make these few hours together everything.

Let's Go, Door County!

Nick Freimuth & the Positive Power of Being

If some people create their own weather,
Nick Freimuth's world is one of perpetual
clear skies, cool breezes, and warm sun,
regardless of formal forecasts
and the minutiae of meteorology.
He's one of those people whose energy
affects the atmosphere of everyone around him,
as he bounds through rooms or bounces
along walkways like a ball seeking a game.
He's always in motion, always promoting
the pleasures of this county we call home.

He's a large man but not imposing, and his voice
is loud but never foreclosing conversations
or the boisterous talk of others drawn to him
like moths to a flame. Whether he's thirsting
for Thursdays or salmon fishing a morning away,
Nick is always quick to share, the band leader
orchestrating the rest of us to join in and play.

There are more than 2300 miles of Door County
but wherever you might be at any given moment,
Nick seems to be there, too, recording it,
reporting it for everyone else to cellphone-see.
He may not know geography, but he knows people,
and the topography of this thumb of land
dipping into the blue of the lake seems
measurably more interesting because of him.

"Let's go, Door County!" might be Nick's catchphrase
(his internet show, too)
but for all of us who follow him
it's really a rallying call to get out there
into the world
and do.

Drift

Today, time is a boat:
A 17-foot Lund with a 90 horsepower Mercury outboard,
four cushioned swivel seats, three of which are occupied,
and a trolling motor on the fritz.
We're fishing the Flats in Sturgeon Bay
on a day perfect for bass and beer.
The sky is sun and the water clear.
In eight to ten feet, the bottom is a shimmering tableau
of sand, rocks, and weeds—all that is necessary
for small mouth to fashion their spawning beds to breed.
A breath of breeze is just enough to push
the boat that carries us in a slow drift
over the tops of these beds, over large male bass
looming in the water protecting their nests
as instinct has decreed, ready to strike
at any living thing threatening, or its like.

My line is in the water, tied to a tube
the color of pumpkin, dragged a half foot over the bottom,
but I half hope my efforts are futile.
My companions and I fish catch-and-release,
hooked by the rush that comes with a hard tug
and the ten-minute fight that might ensue
before we boat the fish, admire it, maybe
snap a cell phone picture or two before returning it
to the lake, followed by another cast
identical to the last, looking for another fish to duel.
But this drift is so seductive and sublime,
and the view of the lakebed so compellingly clear,
I want this moment to extend indefinitely, stay
still as those small mouth bass suspended down there.

Once this drift is over there will be another, and another
after that. We will start up the motor and power back
along the shore, looking to retrace our path
from before. We will cut the motor
and wait for the breeze to catch us, and we will peer
with aging eyes through sun-refracted water
hoping to see what we saw once more;
but everything will have changed from what was,
no matter how hard we try to find it again.
We could work this stretch of lake all afternoon
into evening, vainly searching for something
already gone the moment it was gained.

Stranger in a Strange Poem

for Ralph Murre

He *looks* like a poet, that one—
the Baudelaire hair,
the Whitman whiskers,
the Ginsberg glasses,
the Ferlinghetti chapeau;
the eyes that drink the light in savoring sips,
the grin that promises a chuckle,
soft and low. He's weathered as a fence post
some farmer might have planted decades00 ago,
on land he probably worked one time or another
in a life that meandered from fields to forests,
valleys to plateaus, always thankful for the company
however long it lasted
but restless for more and ready to roll.

You can read the miles in that smile
of all the people he took in on his travels,
who became the music of his verse: The men
he got his hands dirty with, or worse, worked alongside;
the ladies—O, the ladies!—who made everything worthwhile
no matter how long the ride.

You think you know him.
You're sure you've got him pegged.
But then he slides just out of view,
this stranger you were convinced you knew,
to suddenly reappear as someone wholly new:
A singer, a musician, an artist, a friend.

Some of us write poems.
A few are lucky enough to live them.
That one, he *is* a poem.
All you have to do is listen.

Wedding Homily, for Nick and Amanda

March 12, 2015

Some journeys span oceans from shore to shore;
others traverse time in minutes and hours;
there are journeys of steps when we first cross a floor;
journeys within seasons from seedlings to flowers.

We journey through life, each to his own plan,
seeking a sustenance that fulfills in the end
the passions that drive us, both woman and man,
to share our life journeys with one special friend.

Marriage is a journey that begins with a vow—
a promise in words that is made in the heart
through time and space, through then and now—
our journeys will end at the place where we start.

This marriage begins here on this beach,
before those of us gathered to witness and share
the first steps of a journey, as two people reach
for the love and fulfillment their futures will bear.

Next year on this date, and for years after that,
when Nick and Amanda celebrate this day
and recall all the moments, the lean times and fat,
that make up a marriage, I hope they will say
with conviction forged by life's joy and pain,
"I would make this journey with you again."

Wordsmithing

for Rolf

It's not as easy as it looks
Forging words into poems,
Pulling them from the fire
Of the imagination and pounding them
Into sound and syntax
With nothing but the hammers
Of your fingertips striking
The keyboard of the computer

You put a word to the anvil
Of the page, try tapering it to fit
Where you want in line
With other words
Cooling in composition
Shaving letters and syllables
As needed, you never know
When a spark might ignite
A whole new idea
And you're scraping what
You've spent hours on
Back into the cauldron
To begin again

But when you get it right
You can practically smell it in the air
See it on the face, it's there
Something smithed—
Something real—
Something that didn't exist
Before you

With your labor
Made from the molten metal
Of your mind this thing
That you can read
And feel.

Keeping Time

I've lost time.
Lost track of where I left it,
(on a table at home, in a desk at work):
I placed it somewhere for safekeeping,
thinking, *That five minutes will come in handy
later today or early tomorrow*—
Just give me a minute, maybe two,
I'll get back to you in a second...

First, I have to find the time,
but with every turn I take
I keep myself from really keeping
the empty promises I keep making
to waste not/want not what little time I have...

I am the prodigal son who tasted
the time of his life and wasted his time
thinking, he had all the time
in the world to spend, not
knowing he was broke
to begin with in the end.

The Years of Living Vicariously

All the world's a stage, and all the men and women, merely players...
                                        William Shakespeare

At this stage the stage I stand upon
is chaotic and crowded, and I am
one of those stock characters
familiar and avuncular, off to one side
waiting near the wings ready to exit on cue,
then re-enter for the last curtain call,
uncertain all this will come to a close.

My roles have been usurped
by those younger and more virile,
my time near the center of things
as diminished as I sometimes feel.
If the art of living is to live your art,
then I have played that part
to thunderous applause in my head
and felt through others
I have loved and lost and found
the truth that I have borrowed
from the lines that I have read.

Years make careers,
and I've spent mine in costume,
pretending, or trying. I've said
my lines with as much conviction
as rehearsal can provide, but my
best moments were improvised
just to keep momentum from dying,
when scenes took a sudden turn
and someone needed what was

in my power to give by changing
everything I had memorized.

I have no regrets, only reviews.
I've lived many lives vicariously
in the course of living this one, too.
Who knows what anything means
in the mundane moment of things,
so one does what one can
for as long as seems prudent,
then waits for someone else
to give direction, make all those
loose ends seem suddenly congruent.

Running On Beyond

When the end comes
I want to mark mine without punctuation
I want to run on at length
skipping over commas &
ignoring periods
that command me
pause
stop

I want to break all the rules
of mortality and grammar
gerund every noun &
violate verbs of sentient being
in garbled syntax overflowing with meaning
each adjective an exclamation
of declamatory exhilaration
that I declaimed *yes*
I declaim

I will hide in ellipses
and contravene colons
surplus myself in lists of things
I carry forth and follow
to tarry my time
running on beyond
into more &
more &
more (tomorrow)

Playing Dead

I would be a terrible actor, the worst,
the first to be cut from any audition,
if wanting to act was even an ambition.
Thankfully, for the thespian community,
I will never be asked to act.

I wouldn't be cast even to play myself,
I'd be so unconvincing.
That's a fact. I have no timing,
no physical presence to project.
Put me in a scene, even the simplest,
where all I'd have to do is play dead,
what you'd get from me is a stiff performance.

I couldn't even act my age. Other actors
would hate to have to appear next to me,
no doubt about it. I'd forget my lines,
no matter how few, and I'd say something stupid
just to make do. They'd die with me up there,
under the lights with no place to hide,
forced into theatrical suicide
just because of my mummery.

Good thing I've taken to poetry,
where the written word is my stage.
The only dying I do is daily, on the page,
between lines.

"Kapricious"

for Preteen Princesses Everywhere

She's the princess of pout,
there is no doubt,
when she doesn't get her way.

Her face will fall,
her fists will ball,
before she runs away.

She'll disappear,
she'll hide somewhere—
she'll make you call her name.

But this, you see,
is strategy—
it's all part of her game.

You'll wait for her,
then look for her;
you'll search out all her haunts.

Only then will she,
quite icily,
ask you what you want.

Her tone suggests
this injustice
might never be forgiven.

The fault is yours,
you can be sure—
in time, perhaps, forgotten.

What she cedes today,
she seems to say,
will be fiercely fought tomorrow.

Then her mood will shift,
her clouds will lift,
and sunshine soon will follow.

To call Kapri capricious,
fickle and facetious,
is to give the truth to every lie.

She'll dazzle you with smiles,
turn your head with wiles,
then belabor you with questions why.

Just twelve, she wants to seem nineteen,
cocky, moody, sometimes mean,
and ready to take on the world.

Then you catch her in a moment
when doubt becomes self-torment,
and you see she's still your little girl.

Speaking Haiku to 17 Fifth graders

for the kids at Gibraltar Elementary

This is what laureates do,
you've been told:
Bear gifts of words
wrapped in ropes of trope
to eager children
who were promised snacks
of juice packets and Rice Krispies treats
if they pay attention
to the nice man with the beard,
the weird man who speaks in rhyme
some of the time.

Don't worry, you've been assured:
They really *do* like poetry,
and they've never met
a licensed poet before,
one who comes certified
from the County Board
with a pedigree of published books
in his "Read More Poems" bag.
You show them the covers.
One girl asks,
from a yoga position
she has made of herself within her desk,
"Did you really write those?"
You tell her you did
but she doesn't look convinced.

You open one to a random page
and read. Halfway through,

another girl interrupts to ask,
"Are all of them real long?"
You consider an honest response,
but creative lying is the bedrock
upon which creative writing is built
and these young writers
demand truth squeezed into a word,
reduced to the single syllable
of unintelligible sound
that you utter in stutters,
"Uh...uh...uh..."

Seventeen syllables or so of nonsense later,
you are saved by the Club sponsor,
who asks, "Who wants a Rice Krispies?"
to clamorous acclamation.
And that writing activity you planned,
of heroic couplets composed in teams
on a theme of seasonal rebirth?—yeah,
that can wait until after.

It Ain't the Money, Honey

An on-line ad insinuated itself
into my morning e-mail,
and like a raisin in a bowl of rice,
called attention to itself with an insistence
too persistent to ignore:

> *Find out why women prefer men*
> *over 65*, it teased—

and since I was only a cursor-click
away from the answer

(and mired in the dim dog-days
of my 64th year of life)

I bit.
After all, I have a wife.

While the probability 42 years in
she could succumb to the charms
of some sexagenarian Medicare-ready
rake profligate with knowledge
of what women really want
might seem like a long shot,

> *Why take chances when it comes*
> *to mysteries of the human heart...*

(and other vital regions, I say)

> *when a bet on future happiness*
> *can be so simply hedged??*

What I found was this: apparently

> *a man* [my] *age has learned a thing or two*
> *about a thing or two, which women*
> *of all ages find naturally appealing...*

but just as revealing, in a contrary
kind of way, is this *alarming fact*:

> *a woman's libido is waxing*
> *as a man's stamina is waning!!*
> and a *waning stamina*
> *is the first injunction*
> *on the sad, slow spiral*
> *to erectile dysfunction!!!*

However, it doesn't have to be this way:

> *Researchers have found 2 simple,*
> *common nurtrients can turn* [my] *world*
> *around!!!!*

I can be the *stallion* that I once was

> *well into my 70s, medical experts conjecture,*
> *which will make* [me] *irresistible to women*
> *of all ages...*

(despite the receding hairline,
sagging shoulders, and bandy legs
that have effectively put me to pasture).

> *For just three payments of $19.95 each*
> [I] *can live life fully again!*

I can be that guy

women over 65 prefer!
Two little nutrients!
Who knew?

(And here I always thought it was money.)

I wake my sleeping wife
to give her the good news,
share with her

> *the miracle that just $6.95*
> *in shipping and handling will deliver directly*
> *to* [our] *doorstep in 10 to 14 business days!!*

She takes a quick look,
points out the obvious:

"You have to be over 65," she says.
"Go back to sleep."

Killjoy.

Senior Surprises

My body keeps surprising me
every time I bother to give it a gander.
I might be sitting in a lawn chair,
one leg crossed over the other,
chatting up some friend on the phone
or staring off into the neighbor's yard yonder,
when I'll notice how the skin of my leg
has worn so incredibly thin
I can follow the blue lines of veins
mapping their way from my ankle to knee,
a meandering record of my past half-century.
When did they appear?

Or maybe drinking an ice-cold beer
across from friends, here or there,
I'll lift the glass for a sip when suddenly
my shoulder hitches in the socket.
It's damn near all I can do to keep from pouring
half my drink into my pant's pocket.
Talk about embarrassing! What's that about?
When did certain parts of me decide to be
suddenly so cantankerous and difficult?

I know I'm slowing down a bit:
The knees complain when I get up
from a sit, and climbing a flight of stairs
has my lower back talking back in grumbles,
but I never saw this other me coming.
Somewhere back behind my eyeballs is an image
of myself that looks nothing like the guy
discovering an unexplored archipelago
of age spots on the backs of his hands,

mumbling to himself. The guy I like to think I am
isn't knobby knees and knuckles, the schlump
I'm seeing reflected in a store window.
That's got to be an impostor wearing my disguise,
but no—him, I recognize.

Acceptance can be its own surprise.

My Life in Pink

It's what I wore born,
that pink blush of embarrassment
from finding myself the only one naked in the room;
I still wear it every time I am.

It's a giggle, frothy as foam,
bubbling from pink lips;
a gasp of astonishment
receiving your first kiss.

It's sweet carnival candy spun on sticks,
sweeter wedding wine shared in sips,
your sweetest pink, glimpsed:

My pinking life,
Love, (frayed
around the edges, maybe)
is unafraid to be
yours for the shearing.

Tiresias Untuned

My wife says I'm not in tune.
This is a common complaint that has nothing to do with my singing,
which is awful, I confess.
She claims I'm not in tune with *her*—
her moods, *her* thoughts, *her* needs.
She chalks this up to me being a man:
Men just aren't in tune with women, she states
in that way women state things women consider so obvious
you have to be a man to miss them.

I tell her Tiresias was in tune.
He *had* to be in tune.
He was the man punished by the Greek goddess Hera
and transformed on the spot into a woman.
As a woman, Tiresias married and was a mother.
As a woman, Tiresias was beautiful and desired
and could talk to birds, just like Snow White.
Anyone who can talk to birds has to be in tune, I assert
in that way men assert things men consider so incontrovertible
you have to be a woman to disagree with them.

What happened to Tiresias? my wife asks,
dubious about the relevance of his ordeal
but intrigued nevertheless, I think.
He was changed back into a man, I say.
After seven years living as a woman, Tiresias steps on some snakes
or doesn't step on some snakes in a garden—
the details are kind of murky, this being Greek mythology—
and is rewarded by the gods and immediately transformed
back into a man. *He goes on to become one of the great Greek prophets
and experts on female sexuality,* I add,
figuring this conclusively proves my point.

Yeah, I bet he does, she says, shaking her head
in that head-shaking way women use to show just how clueless men can be.
Seven years a woman, and that gives him the keys to the queendom?
Snakes and birds? Only a man would believe a story like that.

She walks away trilling something princess-y
from Disney—in tune, of course—leaving the legacy of poor Tiresias
to me, tuneless as a man can be.

The Opposite of Sex

I dreamed I woke this morning female from the outside in.
The lumbering man of lumpen sensibilities
who'd gone to bed the night before
morphed through magic into something familiar
but completely beyond the experience of what I'd been.
A spill of hair fine as corn silk fell across my face
from a head whose hirsute days had long since passed,
and the beard that had defined my jaw and chin
had been replaced by skin, soft and free of scratch.
Hairless, too, were my shoulders and my chest,
which suddenly felt centered in a way that shocked me awake:
I had breasts my hands could fully cup, and further down
between my legs—an absence more profound than empty space.

I lay as still as stone beneath the quilts, trying to assess
what had happened since last night, looking for reason
to explain a transformation too illogical to comprehend.
Like Tiresias, that hapless Greek of ancient myth,
had I transgressed in some manner great or small?
Misused my male privilege in some thoughtless way,
leveraged an advantage that wasn't mine, meant or not?
Or was I wrong to think being remade a woman punishment at all?
What if this were *reward* for something I'd recently done,
some selfless service to others that proved I was ready
to be more than just a man? As a woman would I find
a sense of being that could help me understand
the elemental purpose of what it means to be alive—
and love—and live—in the time I have at hand?

I felt a stirring next to me: My wife surfacing from sleep.
My breath caught in my chest, wondering her reaction
to what she'd soon perceive. Would she recoil in horror,

shake her head in disbelief? Scramble from the bed,
race from the room, seek shelter somewhere,
scream for help, phone the police?
Or would she choke back laughter after examining my face,
perhaps throw the covers back to see if this were some joke,
an elaborate deceit that would make sense to her
once it was revealed?

When she did none of those things, I risked venturing
a look, uncertain what I'd see. Would she, too, have changed,
transformed into an approximation of me: balding head,
wispy beard, narrow hips and knobby knees?
Unlike me, she seemed to be herself still, much the same she was
from what she was the night before, and all the nights before that
we had lain together in this bed. She was the woman,
once the girl, I'd fallen in love with and wed. Friend, lover,
confidant, mother—she was the person who knew me best.
How could she forgive me *this* betrayal, so essentially physical,
beyond infidelity—the opposite, in fact, of sex?

She surprised me: She yawned.
Smiled.
Reached a hand out.
Touched my head.

Her fingers felt electric.
I could have died in the moment.
I woke up instead.

Forensic Analysis

I leave something of myself in everything I write.
A piece of me here or there,
slipping between letters into white
or dripping like spatter
into the inky abyss of type.
I lose a little of me to get things really right.

Once I'm into a poem, I'm in it for life.
I can glimpse myself buried in the lines.
You may sense me sliding behind
a metaphor or hiding in a rhyme.
I'm there somewhere lurking in syntax,
the criminal at his crime.

I imagine as I'm writing
the poem is proof I lived.
Long after I'm dust and done
these words will somehow give
a clue of who I was when I was
doing what I did.

Maybe I'll live forever in those pieces that I hid.

3

What a Poem Can Do

We've all seen what a word can do
by itself, left to its own inflections:
it can get you killed,
start a war,
end

everything in a heartbeat;
everything gone in a breath.

What a poem can do is different:
it can wrangle words
deadly as bullets and bombs
and corral them into blooms of flowers
instead; it can line them up in love,
let them beat in feet of rhythm
regular as blood-
bringing life,
begin

everything in a heartbeat;
everything born in a breath.

The Misuse of Silence

Things left unsaid speak sometimes most loudly
when words refuse to form themselves as such;
and silence in its stead echoes profoundly,
while what was left unsaid resounds too much.

I have hidden behind such silence, but not proudly;
it is an art that I mastered when I was young.
The things I left unsaid spoke for me roundly
when I swallowed words I meant and bit my tongue.

Eating Our Own

My son now looks like me
when I was his age,
as I now look like my dad
when he was mine.

This is Nature's way,
apparently.

We become what held us
(in time)
inherently:

the arms
that lifted us to float
impossibly in the air;
the eyes
that imagined what we
could become
(in time)
with care.

We become
the voice,
the walk,
the build,
the skin,
the hair.

We become what's next
in line,

by digesting,
by divesting
the virus of ourselves
we share

(in time).

Patience and the Pain of Becoming

Pain is hard to bear...but with patience,
day by day, even this will pass away.
—Theodore Tilton

I learned patience by becoming
one: An unfortunate fall left me
nursed, needful of the ministrations of others;
watchful, waiting for the energy of any activity
to envelope me in its backwash.

Minutes matter again.
Time defines itself, one tick at a time:
"Take your time," I hear.
"There's plenty of time," I'm told.
"Just be patient."
"Time heals."
I burrow into the marrow of each moment,
mindful of silences, sounds.

Patience is a feminine virtue:
if you're a man, you find that out
by becoming the furniture
of whatever room you occupy,
a fixed point in the geography
that others need to negotiate
as they move with the currents
of the day: arriving, departing
(when and if) stopping, starting
and always tantalizingly just beyond reach.

When you are truly patient,
I have learned,

an empty hand isn't.
It is waiting patiently to be filled.
And pain will pass (eventually)
if you're patient.

Grief

An Elegy for Buddy

Mornings are worst.
I wake in half-light
and ache for the routine of you
to help me fill the hours.
I still expect to see you here—
the black fluff of a pup
who grew into such a handsome dog.
The house is the same
but it is different
without you.
The places I once looked for you
are empty of you
but the sense of you remains,
a pang too sharp to endure and
too precious to surrender.

There, around the corner of a farther room,
waiting patiently for my approach—
Here, in a hallway,
shrouded in shadow,
your brown eyes luminous
with love—

Some say pets are practice
for greater grief to come,
an abscess of absence
only time can dull
and distance displace.

If so, my beautiful boy,
your work here is done.
My heart, thus broken,
is numb.

Reductive Reasoning

It takes two to make one.
Thirty-six weeks, more or less,
to add another to the family fold.
New, most weigh in under ten pounds
but pack a whopping thirty-seven trillion cells
into a body that won't get much taller than a shrub,
once it gets old.

It takes years to properly grow one,
and thousands of dollars, millions maybe,
to fully prepare one for life,
providing a range of possibilities
of how one's story might be told
through the many minutes, hours, days, and months
of cultivation it requires to make the one
the world will behold.

It takes one bullet,
costing about three cents,
just a split second,
hardly measurable in time,
to reduce all that everything
to nothing.
Kill it cold.

Prepositions of Grief

for Mason Potter (2000-2021)

From moment to moment the After is worse
than the During waiting/grieving
when a bullet blasts out of nowhere/somewhere
to crack a skull like an eggshell breaking.
And what was once a twenty-one-year-old
man-child effervescent with life
in all its fizzy possibilities
is rendered defunct/brain dead
kept in suspension between worlds
by marvelous medical machinery
that will be rolled into the next room
(into the next tragedy) once his parents decide
to say their goodbyes/pull the plug.

The During doesn't allow for much more than doing
the things that need to be done
moment by moment in the time that allows
(the sharing/the asking/the explaining/the caring)
knowing that the Waiting might be the best of what is left
as the doctors/the nurses/the police/the press
probe/piece together the broken bits of what has happened
when answers seem like something
to hold to as a substitute for hope.

The After doesn't do time in whirls of motion/emotion
swirling in a frenzy of feeling as the During does.
The After slows the clock to a crawl that suddenly stops.
And what was once there (to have/to hold/to touch/to love)

is a yawning memory empty of reality/absent of space
reduced to things that no longer matter to one no longer there
(the clothes/the shoes/the toiletries/the trinkets)
the inconsequential but vitally important things
that once added up to a living person/living each moment
taken for granted/granted those moments
theirs for the keeping by virtue of being someone
summarily subtracted/redacted by a gun
one that fit so snugly in somebody else's
arbitrarily extended adolescent hand.

Sleep, a Lullaby

for John A. Orlock (April 6, 1924 – October 13, 2010)

You woke this morning hollow from
the struggle just to rise,
by half the man you were last year
but twice the man in need.
The heart that beat so sure and strong
in cadence to your step,
now whispered that the time had come
for you to close your eyes.

The life you lived was fully filled
with moments in full flow
outside the walls you built around
the dreams you locked away.
The things you set aside from others
were things most never saw,
a part of you you kept distilled
for only you to know.

And now that you have hollowed out
a place inside to keep
the things you culled from all the things
you found along the way,
you stand before the last unknown
made known through one last dream:
So, close your eyes and calm your doubt
and sleep, my Father, sleep.

Assignment

I live as if this life is mine to waste;
I squander time and seasons without thought.

The trees around the block on which I live
are dressed in sun-drenched colors red and orange;
but I see things in only black and white
and race from one assignment to the next,
consumed with worries trivial and vain
without the sense to pause and take a look
at all the things around me that I've missed.

The sky above, a bowl of blue so vast
eternity itself could swim within,
invites a plunge into its autumn depths
to float away with time to contemplate
the path my life has taken up to now.

But I persist perseverating what
for me is nothing more than idle talk.
The things that matter most to me are lost
because like some I've lacked the will to be
that man who can embrace the ones he loves
and call them out by name for them to hear.

Instead, I sit here struck like some dumb beast,
chewing words I yearn to say but can't.

* * *

My father died on Wednesday early morn,
the night made darker by a passing storm
that tipped October's balmy southern winds
with arrowheads of rain and seeping chill.

The sun that rose next day was cold but bright,
the morning shadows longer in new light—
And I had one assignment left to write
without the skill to make myself less trite.

John

Upon Passing

There was no mistaking him:
Gentle giant,
bear-hug of a man.
Teacher, preacher
of patience and listening,
amused by the daily doing
of opening minds
to the possibilities
present in sorting through
the choices there for each of us
to find.

He always led with a laugh,
a deep eruption of genuine joy,
followed with a helping hand.
He was first a fast friend
and last a kind man,
the kind of man who makes
the world a more interesting place
just by being there.

Don't call this poem a eulogy.
John's passing
isn't an ending
since his presence
was so defined:
Plant his memory
in the back of your mind,
wait for him to bloom.

He'll be there
(somewhere)
filling every room.

About Bill

October 23, 1957 — February 6, 2013

What I remember most is the stillness, Bill:
In a room full of moving bodies
charting seasonal celebrations and commemorations,
you were a fixed point on the periphery
of family frenzy, standing slightly forward
on the balls of your feet, a bemused smile
flirting with the corners of your mouth;
or sitting off to the side, a baby on your lap
or someone's child riding your knee.

That was the happiest I ever saw you, Bill:
Your smile was bright enough to fill the room,
warm enough to make weather,
but you weren't one to call attention to yourself.
You seemed most a part of things *apart*
from everyone else, a man of few words
whose favorite expression was a shrug.
You were the man who wasn't there
even when you were.

The cliché holds that still waters run deep,
but if your depths were your own, Bill,
concealing secrets none but you would know,
you were still a reservoir for those
you left behind. Perhaps we saw
reflected in your calm surface
what we wanted to see, missing what
was really roiling beneath. Maybe we mistook
your quiet for calm.

I want to think that in those last moments, Bill,
as you relinquished yourself to the silence
that was your constant companion,
you found that which you could not find.
Our world will continue to spin
without you: Things don't stop
just because you stepped off into eternity.
Know, though, there is a hole in the rooms
you once occupied, impossible to fill.

Bedouins

My mother-in-law at eighty-nine,
good German-Irish woman she,
devoted Roman Catholic
living the American plan
with grace recited over meals
during each course of the day,
unexpectedly is
but perplexedly now
a Bedouin.

A misplaced step unfolding herself
from bed one morning past
resulted in a displaced hip,
and the house she has called home
for fifty years is suddenly treacherous,
precarious as a pitching ship:
no practical way for a woman
with her legs to navigate four levels
and three flights of stairs
(basement to bedroom)
in unincorporated suburbia, no less,
so her children have had to do
in conference calls across the country
what she once daily did—decide
where next to pitch her tent
to live the remainder of her days
a Bedouin.

Two weeks with one,
a week with another,
maybe a month with us
if the dining room off the kitchen

can be converted
into a makeshift oasis
with a rented hospital bed,
once her brittle old bones heal
sufficiently to move her.
Still, all these plans, all these
contingencies are avoidance—
the central dilemma
merely delayed, not resolved:
where does Mom go to live
what time remains her
now that time has made her
a Bedouin?

Assisted living?
What once we called "old folks"
homes, low-slung low-profile
buildings that somewhat resemble
apartments without, hospitals within,
where daily life is reduced to a routine of
scheduled activities,
scheduled meals,
scheduled therapies,
interrupted only by
unscheduled departures
and new arrivals:
a terminal for the terminal,
more or less, for those
without good fortune or family
to stay placed within
the places they know.

This isn't what we had in mind
for Mom, we say;
that isn't what we imagine

for ourselves someday.
Somehow when we get to thinking
of cashing in our golden years,
what we're buying isn't *this*;
but what to do in the mean times
when an untimely step precedes
a precipitous fall,
that between times upends
everything,
making Bedouins of us all?

Being Betty

June 19, 1927—November 12, 2017

She was the center of every room.
If she was sitting in a corner, that corner
became the center—not because of theatrics
or a booming voice or a personality
the size of a stage. Her talent wasn't drawing
attention to herself, it was inviting
a person she didn't know to share a moment
sketching out stories about little things
that her interest in made fascinating,
and soon there would be a coterie
in orbit around her, as bright
with reflective light as the moon.

Betty wasn't big with big gestures:
A waggle of her shoulders was all she'd do
for dancing, regardless of the tempo
or tune. She had an easy laugh
that was just as easily self-directed,
especially in those times with family
or friends when something she said
or did got teased: she was good
rolling with punchlines, being the joke,
letting you know with a slight wave
all that ribbing left her pleased.

Betty's life like most lives was a road
more roundabout than straight.
Hers had its share of unlucky detours,
sudden swerves, but she never lost
the pleasure of the journey,

never doubled back because of fright.
She learned to lean into every curve
over 90 years of living,
loving what needed loving in the flow—
her family in all its extensions,
seven children,
thirteen grandchildren,
eleven great grandchildren—
a long legacy of life she left in leaving us,
true to her own way, on a Sunday
morning meant now for mourning,
simple as sitting down and letting go.

4

If William Carlos Williams Lived My Life

much more depends
upon

the yellow Conquest
pencils

wrapped in green
rubber bands

beside the test
booklets.

Trippy

after Carl Sandburg's "Chicago"

> Couch-crowder of the family room,
> toy-destroyer, snack-stealer,
> howling hound in a quiet house;
> sneak-hider of shoes
> and thief-collector of wayward socks.

They said you would be lanky, and I believe them now for I have seen you stretch out longer than an awkward moment on the floor beneath my feet;

They told me you would be lazy, and I know this to be true, for I have watched whole afternoons collapse around you while you whiled hours away snout to tail in a dream state, rousing yourself only long enough to eat;

And they warned me you were fast, your greyhound genes the pedigree for your sudden bursts of speed, crossing a field in pursuit of some prize only you could see, despite our panicked commands to heel and retreat;

But I have known you too these many years as a faithful friend, whose eyes never judge me for the mistakes I daily make, whose affections never waver no matter how the day might break.

> Licking,
> Drooling,
> Scratching,
> Shedding,

Rude wet-nosed sniffer of butts you might in many ways be, but you are so much part of the furniture of our lives now, our home will seem empty when you leave us, loping off into memory.

Stopping by Daffodils on a Chilly Evening, or

A Word's Worth of Frost in Mid-May

I wandered, aimless, through yellow woods
searching for diverging roads;
and when I found two, long I stood
wondering where the hell I was.

I walked down one as far as I could
to where it emptied in a vale,
and there, beside a lake and trees,
I spied a host of daffodils.

They danced and twirled in the breeze,
and sorry I could not dawdle there
to watch them wink with bud and leaves
at any cloud that might pass o'er.

A woods' worth of poetic trope
couldn't do justice to this scene
of jocund flowers, trees, and birds
beside a lake with waters green.

But night was coming, and with it frost;
I had miles of walking still ahead.
I thought I might return next day,
but those daffodils would soon be dead.

I'm sure I'll mourn them with a sigh,
sometime ages and ages whence
they flash upon my inward eye,
which is the bedrock of experience:

Some flowers died but I survived,
and that has made all the difference.

Thirteen Ways of Looking at a Gun

with due apologies to Wallace Stevens

I
Among twenty snow swept houses,
the only sound heard
was the click of a gun.

II
I was of three dispositions,
like a cabinet
in which there are kept three guns.

III
A gun can make masculine
even the most feminine hand.

IV
A man needs a gun
as a woman needs a gun.
A gun doesn't discriminate
against either one.

V
I can never decide:
Do I prefer the pop
of a small caliber pistol,
or the percussive pow
of a semi-automatic assault rifle?
Which resounds longer
after?

VI

A woman's fingers
were made to fondle
the barrel of a gun;
red nail polish looks best
against blue-black
glistening steel.

VII

(Was the previous verse
too loaded with Freudian repercussions?
Did Freud ever experience in hand
the heft of a Sig Sauer p365
held, hugely satisfying?)

VIII

I know the rhythms of rounds
and the unmistakable sounds
of varied voices, raised.
A gun speaks all languages
by speaking one.

IX

When a gun is used,
God rejoices that Man has used
His greatest gift—freedom
to choose, as guaranteed
by the Second Amendment.

X

At the sight of a gun
scattering a crowd of celebrants,
even the most courageous
will cower in confusion.

XI

A gun is just a tool,
I've been told,
no better or worse than any other
in the shed. Unlike a shovel,
however, a gun can fire a projectile
at 1700 miles per hour,
whereas the fastest shovel
can throw dirt several feet,
perhaps.

XII

A gun at rest
is no more lethal than a shovel,
so says the gunsmith.

XIII

A shovel is more useful
than a gun for digging a hole.
A gun is more useful
than a shovel for giving a reason
for digging a hole.

5

Earth Day Elegy, 2022

We've made the world a woman,
named Earth our Mother;
exalted her, celebrated her
for giving birth to all things living
that crawled from her waters
and grew from her soils.

We've spent countless words writing
of her many moods—
her sanguine spells of tranquility,
her tempestuous turns of volatility,
in storms sometimes so violent we cower
in prayers of deliverance
that we might be spared her wrath
to once more bask
in the essence of her soothing calm.

We've pledged our love everlasting
in numberless songs and psalms,
ceremonies and scriptures,
thanking her for the fecundity
born from her bucolic generosity
that nourishes us in all seasons.

And we have whispered manifold
endearments of fidelity and affection
each time we have used her
for reasons of our own pleasure,
promising her next time
we will be better, we will make amends,
tend to the needs of her existence

in equal measure to our own;
and we will love her as we do ourselves,

even as we kill her.

Upon Reading the Marshall Islands Are Sinking

for the people I met there 1992-1994

I dream of writing these islands, green and white,
strung like beads on a bracelet of an atoll
dangling in the blue Pacific of memory,
in waters that reach to embrace them
from below, to pull them from sun and sky
into an oblivion dark and deep.

I say their names in my sleep: Kwajalein, Ebeye,
Bigej, Eniwetak, Roi-Namur—each a slice
of coral, sand, and rock flat as a stone worn smooth
by washing waves that ceaselessly roll ashore,
these islands little more than an afterthought
in the vast sweep of the ocean.

Volcanoes created them but man unkind
broke them, blasting them with bombs and missiles,
nuclear tests and Star Wars systems, rendering some
unlovable, others unlivable, scoured of what
few trees and flowers naturally grew there
and the indigenous people who called them home.

A warming world threatens now to swallow them whole,
to erase a piece of tropic tranquility few maps
even bother to mark, to displace a people and a culture
older than empires, casting thousands of Marshallese
into exile none of them expected, into refugee camps
in far-flung places few of them can imagine.

When the Marshalls disappear, who will remember
such a tiny, insignificant nation whose land mass is smaller
than Milwaukee, sprinkled over thousands of miles of ocean?
Who will care there was ever such a place, where to write
of these islands is to dream them, white and green,
floating like lotus blossoms on the swells of the Pacific?

Eight Top Species Threatened by Climate Change

A Featured Headline in Care2News

1. Pity the poor Pacific bearded seal,
someday he'll be shaved from existence.

2. Say goodbye to the buzz of tropical bees,
conspicuous soon for their silence.

3. Wear your worry for the Waved Albatross,
about to be shot from the sky.

4. Cheer your last for the Baltimore Orioles,
the ones that really do fly.

5. *Hooroo*, Northern Hairy-Nose Wombat,
maybe someday you will be missed.

6. So long, North American Pika,
may your passing be painless and swift.

7. Give a hug to the powerful polar bear,
at least those outside of a zoo.

8. But grieve not for the ape called Human,
who will be getting what he is due.

A Poem for My Conservative Friends

I know who you are. I feel your pain.
A multitude of months and counting, still reeling from the "stealing,"
barely surviving all that Covid conniving, living under the yoke of a woke mob
of ruthless do-gooders and progressively minded socialist scientists,
subject to the whims of a Squad of civil sadists intent on enacting for their own pleasure
a measure of revenge in the reforms of governmental norms they have legislated
(in which health care, the environment, racial equality, and education
have been prioritized at the expense of cutting taxes and gashing regulations,
caging migrant families and subverting vaccinations)
all at your expense, no less, my conservative neighbors and friends!
Fear not, the polls predict your living nightmare will soon end.
No talk of building back better, no record number of jobs created,
can compensate for the horrors of receiving federal pandemic relief!
No grand bargain on infrastructure will ever rebuild the bridges burned
investigating an insurrection fomented by the previous Commander-in-Chief!
Your deliverance in the Midterms, practically guaranteed,
is nigh at hand—there!
Isn't that Kevin McCarthy upon a galloping steed,
riding to your rescue, rallying a posse of the best and bravest
cultural warriors this country so desperately needs? A Renaissance of Republicanism
seems certainly in the offing, led by a "Magnificent Seven" of noble statesmen
and stateswomen, whose names virtually roll off the tongue into legend:
Lauren Boebert, Madison Cawthorn, Louis Gohmert, Jimmy Jordan,
Marjorie Taylor Greene, Mo Brooks, Matty Gaetz, Paul Gosar—wait! That's *eight!*
A cohort of constitutional scholars like this country has never seen!

Each a paragon of virtue, a profile in patriotism,
embracing the best of Truth*iness*, Justice*ness*, and the Authoritarian Way!
And I've not even talked about the Senate yet.
Doesn't that serve to brighten your day?
Just thinking thoughts of Mitch McConnell once again in charge
should reignite your sodden spirit with inflamed inspiration!
If that isn't balm for your Gileads, my Q-conditioned compatriots,
then there truly is no mitigation from the vile ministrations of Nancy Pelosi
and the soul-grinding governance of Joe Biden, who had the temerity,
the shameless audacity, to accept the Electoral College results without complaint.

Still doubt my sincerity?
Let's Go, Brandon! There. I've said it.
Want more? Trump/Trump 2024.
(Now there's a poem you can write to me, just like the time before.)

Moving Closer to a Distant Reality

The sky overhead is a limitless void
made bracingly blue by a cold sun
indifferent to either horizon;

on one side of the world
Japan crumbles into ocean fissures,
disappearing under black water;

on the other side
blood gushes like oil on North African sands
while a butterfly beats its wings;

I am stuck in between
staring into congealing yolk and a smear of butter
as disaster segues into erectile dysfunction;

the waitress warms my coffee with a smile
that invites nothing more than a smile in return
and conjures the check from a pocket in her apron,

slides it with practiced efficiency
to a clean spot on the Formica tabletop, upside down,
where it smiles up at me from cursive curlicues—

"Have a great day!!!" it reminds me.
Underlined for emphasis,
punctuated with urgency lest we all forget:

Somewhere distant door chimes ring;
Angels await their wings when
God gets back from break.

The Dead of War Speak Their Piece in Silence

Language no longer separates them as it does the living.
The dead have no need for alphabets:
English vowels, Cyrillic consonants, Chinese pictographs—
all are useless for what they have to say.
Words don't mean anything, spoken or scripted.
To the dead they are the same.
They are noise that fills a void,
a volume that drains understanding from the world,
that keeps their truth from being heard.

The living love words, *their* words,
barked and brayed, written and repeated.
Words are candy they let dissolve in their mouths,
flavoring every sentence with sweet sincerity
even they sometimes believe. They string them
into beautiful colloquies and passionate proclamations,
plain-spoken platitudes and direct declarations.
Words are weapons, brandished like swords.
Marched and paraded, they can explode and engulf
millions of people once more in war.

The living make walls of words from war
to hide behind for protection.
The dead of war speak their piece in silence,
simply, without circumspection.

Deconstructing Kyle Rittenhouse

He'll be in pieces before the ink on the verdict is dry.
He'll be cut-up, packaged, and available in sound bites,
perfect for cocktail parties and caucus cookouts.
He'll be silk-screened and memed on tee shirts
and ball caps; you'll find him here and there,
wherever perishables are sold at discount.
He'll be broken down and reassembled every time
someone shoots his mouth off about the first,
the second, the fourth, or the fifth and the inalienable
right to kill others who get too close.

He'll be ground into powder and packed into expletives.
He'll be splattered in newsprint the next time
some pudgy Proud Boy wannabe plays Charles Bronson
on city streets overrun with angry imbeciles
packing heat. You want your Kyle fresh-faced
and cooked to order? You better hurry: America
likes new meat field dressed and cut to the bone bloody,
and tomorrow's Kyle is already out there somewhere,
just itching to pull the trigger.

The Perks of Burning Books in South Dakota

Rapid City School District Considering Book Destruction
          Headline Out of Sioux Falls, S.D. (Keloland News)

The five books earmarked for destruction are *The Circle* by Dave Eggers;
How Beautiful We Were: A Novel by Imbolo Mbue;
Fun Home: A Family Tragicomic by Alison Bechdel;
Girl, Woman, Other: A Novel by Bernardine Evaristo;
and *The Perks of Being a Wallflower* by Stephen Chbosky.

Burning isn't banning, the Board will have you know.
They're not into "banning" books, they're into *destroying* them.
It's a yearly thing, similar to trees shedding their leaves.
Incinerate the old to clear shelf space for the new,
or just shelf space since South Dakota is noted for its open spaces,
as anyone who's ever driven the state can tell you.

These five books have undergone a "rigorous review,"
as all books in Rapid City have and do. Young minds are too much
like unmade beds, and it's for the Board to decide what linens to use.
Reading is overrated—and sometimes dangerous too.
Too many different ideas can be threatening to the well-made mind.
Besides, how ya' spoz'ta keep 'em in Dakota once they've read about gay
     Paree?

Supremely Courted, a Judicious Review

Our Founding Fathers famously,
fulsome in philosophy,
fluent in apostasy,
designed a court specifically
to check religiosity
from infecting legislation passed
affecting the whole nation lest
the commonwealth they prized most dear
descend in chaos, strife, and fear
(with prudent, secular, reasoned speech
abridged by dogma's overreach).

The court they crafted and equipped
would protect the public from such trysts
as could occur when weak-willed men,
imprudently placed in government,
might find themselves seduced by skanks
and evangelical mountebanks.

What they couldn't anticipate,
their thirteen colonies fifty states,
was a court of judges picked and packed
by the moneyed muscle of partisan flacks
(whose purpose wasn't jurisprudence, per se,
but judgments intended to go their way).

This Court has become, through stealth and steal,
nine women and men in robes that conceal
the interests that own the decisions they make
which determine the laws of give and take.
And what was once supremely sported
in the even hand of justice comported

(the trust of the public in what was done)
is lost in the service of serving some.

Their recent opinions, ruefully reported,
rendered on scales tipped by thumbs,
are decisions so suspect *they* should be aborted
before Justice, blind, is also struck dumb.

The Adulting of Rebecca Kleefisch

In an interview with the Milwaukee Journal Sentinel, Kleefisch said her approach to COVID-19, if elected governor, would be "trusting adults to do their own adulting."

Of all the various mandates applied,
of testing, tracing, and masking inside,
of school shutdowns and zooming to work,
experimental treatments (some quite berserk),
dispensing vaccines as if they were candy,
debunking lies with all the facts handy,
tabulating costs of this horrid disease,
in dollars and deaths and social unease,

Rebecca Kleefisch has seized this moment
to offer her remedy to end the torment
caused by COVID and its vile variants:
She'll win over anti-vaxxer adherents
by trusting adults to do their "adulting"
without doubting decisions or defaulting
if those decisions, adulted or otherwise,
cost the state a few thousand more lives.

"Freedom" (and winning) is worth any COVIDing:
On that you can trust, Rebecca ain't kidding.

Trump's Big Lie

The Big Lie is built from all His little lies,
stuck together like barnyard straw and shit
(and all the more redolent because of it):

The Big Lie wants to erase
all who came before Him, to tell us
less of *them* means more of Him,
and what we once held self-evident
is corruption, vile and pestilent
(because all patriots deceived
know what they once believed
is as false as He is true):

The Big Lie maintains
only He knows the Truth
(and should reap the rewards that accrue
from telling it):

The Big Lie demands repetition.
Lie loudly. Believe bigly
(and give, always give):

The Big Lie is a wholly owned subsidiary
of Trump International
(available everywhere
bullshit is bought and sold).

Writing Out Loud in America

Shush, some advise,
those who prefer their poetry in genteel tones
with a finger to its lips.
There is noise enough in this world.
Verse shouldn't make things worse.
Impudent prose already abides.
Rather a poem should soothe than stir,
sedate than arouse, with words
that float like birds on the tides.
Write softly in whispers, they say.
Sidle, don't stride.

But today, June 24, more than a fifth
of the way through the twenty-first century,
is a day for clamor and cacophony,
for raised voices and bellicose stridency,
for shrill and cry, for bedlam and shout,
for words that erupt in riot and rout.
For when social contracts fall to deviancy,
when rights are revoked for the sake of expediency,
when partisan politics pollute the Commonwealth
and laws are sanctioned that compromise health,
a poem must in trust roar out in rage,
should lift itself literally up from the page,
be rudely insistent impolitic banter,
while words (what they're worth)
still mean,
still matter.

Lost in Grammarica

After my pronouns defected,
choosing to render gender moot,
pulling point-of-view
up by the root, my nouns
decided to follow suit and abandon
all pretense of person, place, or thing,
leaving me to guess the names
of things again, common or proper.

Thinking became treacherous,
speech a conversation stopper.
What once was classifiable,
definable and assignable,
was now a game of gauging
what was politically viable
within the shifting landscape
of the socially certifiable.

When grammar grovels
at the feet of fashion,
and rules reorient themselves
to the current passion,
then language loses liquidity
as discourse is drained of currency,
until communication itself collapses
and what fills the void
is the braying of asses.

If silence is the sane alternative
to the risk of being thought pejorative,
cancel my culture now.
The only sounds worth making then
won't even be words anyhow.

6

Expressing (Trains in Four Tracks)

1
Something about a train is
both marvelous and mundane,
the ways it thunders along trails of track
like a symphony composed of percussion and clang,
the clickity clack of its wheels transfixing
those of us awed by its length and strength,
while others just wait, patient for its passing,
in order to resume pedestrian journeys again.

2
Trains overwhelm in ways wonder once did
when the world was a chaotic cacophony
of sounds, with sights bright as steel
and smells dense as diesel; crossings
used to signal something significant then,
in the progress of a day, for those anxious
for something swift to carry them away.

3
I love the disruptive ways of a train,
the anticipation of it in the distance,
its Cyclops eye blinking and winking
through haze of heat or fog of cold
as it powers forth drawing ever closer,
until at once it is upon then past,
blasting a triumphal note of resolve
racing to a destination I always imagine
far more interesting than my own.

4

Something about a train speaks to what was
in ways an airplane or automobile never could:
They are of air and asphalt, soaring,
circling, curving, and swerving,
modern conveyances of speed and convenience.
A train, however, is iron rammed through country
in all its wild beauty, an invitation
to everything I dreamed I might someday see,
running on rails straight into horizons
on an express line that stopped for me.

Old Goat, Scrounging
(A Self-Assessment of Sorts)

I feel less poet than bearded goat some days.
I scribble and scrounge among a detritus of words
scattered in mind, blind, decidedly the ninny
who can't quite hold on to an idea worth keeping
longer than it takes to fumble it away.

I chew my cud in quantity, convinced
more than a mouthful will yield something worthwhile,
something worth the swallow, but I lose the taste
of what I think I want to say, and what I'm left with
is the hollow feeling that all this time has been a waste.

I've eaten my words too many times to count,
and the few good things I've spit out
in the course of composing some days
wouldn't confuse anyone of art,
regurgitated or otherwise.

That's the maddening thing mucking about a poem:
You bite into an idea, thinking, *This is some gourmet stuff!*
Who wouldn't want a chunk of this?
While your gut is grumbling, *This junk? Who are you kidding?*
Still, you keep gnawing until all that gnawing ends in this.

Satisfying Conclusions

What we have is what we get,
with endings not quite scripted yet.

We overlap in scenes of time,
rehearsing cues, reciting lines,

our days a progress meant to seem
as seamless as a waking dream.

We move together, or apart,
in measured steps that stop and start

in syncopation with each other,
to exit cleanly, without bother.

From the wings we watch and wait,
our curtain call as sure as fate

or February with its cutting cold
and nights made new for feeling old.

Still, we move (it's that or rust),
each day a play in loving trust.

We know too well too soon we'll quit.
Our ending's not been written yet.

Practical(ly) Poetry

I want this poem to be practical,
as useful as a five-dollar bill;
you can carry it (folded)
in a wallet or purse
(it will pocket quite nicely
with other, less practical,
varieties of verse).

I wrote it to be parenthetical
(there for you whenever
you need it to be):
Perhaps in a bar,
you're sipping a drink;
talk turns as talk does
(quite naturally)
to the state and fate of modern poetry,
with everyone shouting what they think.

Maybe somebody mentions cummings
(or Whitman or Merwyn or Frost).
Someone else lobs couplets of Pope like grenades,
and the place suddenly explodes into verse.
You won't have to duck for cover.
You can stand your ground
with the worst.
You can take out this poem
from wherever it's kept, from
a pocket or wallet or purse.

You unfold it with such deliberate care,
quiet settles like fog on the room.
Everyone's curious what you have there.

That's when this poem's usefulness
(its *raison d'etre*) will open itself like a bloom.

It's for moments like this that I wrote it,
when the world hangs on a word;
when expectations are there to be met
and fulfilled, distilled
into choice nouns and verbs.

Go ahead and read it out loud;
you can read what I've just written
here. You can let these words
loose like caged birds
(their practical purpose is clear).

A spirited reading of what's in your hand,
finessed with style and caressed
with command, delivered
with conviction and concluded
with a wink, should result in this
outcome: This poem for a drink?

...Or this poem and a five-dollar bill?

Word Wastrel: A Life Devised in Four Stanzas

I grew up in a time when taciturn was in.
The Duke, Clint, Bronson, McQueen
were men of action and scant word-work,
emulated for their lack of verbiage
in a world awash with talk and complex sentences.
They squeezed syllables into silence,
steely and lethal, and when they squinted,
their eyes spoke volumes. My friends and I
studied the look, trying on various moods
of terse masculinity in preparation for the day
when we could bottle personality
into Molotov cocktails of mum manliness.

How strange that my personality soon evolved
in ways voluble and verbose. In college
I modeled the manic mutterings of Woody Allen.
I effervesced with bubbly conversation
and nonstop repartee. There wasn't a pregnant pause
I wasn't keen to abort with a comment or joke,
filling every gap with observation and play-by-play.
I awoke each morning with a mouthful of words
restless for release, buzzing to burst from my lips
like a soliloquy of liberated bees.
I wasn't just garrulous, I was logorrheic
in ways an auctioneer might admire.
And if what I said from sentence to segue
made no sense, I was never deterred:
My stream-of-conscious commentary
continued to flow in flash floods of prolixity
too torrential to avoid.

By the muddle of my middle years,
when career and family considerations
curtailed the rambling discourse of my youth
in favor of more measured declarations,
I became Tom Hanks in modulated erudition.
I chose my words with the care a sommelier
selects a particular vintage to complement
the finest fare, and what was once boisterous
and absurd had become, in a word, reserved.
I was a paragon of verbal restraint and contemplation,
each syllable weighed judiciously for audience
interpretation so as not to offend or preclude
any and all from convivial participation.
You can imagine the indigestion I experienced
on a continual basis of not only having to bite my tongue
in good taste, but to swallow my words
when I so wanted to spit them out! I was tormented
until retirement by acute expressive constipation.

Now that I approach the onset of caducity,
I am like Anthony Hopkins sans lucidity,
raging against the vagaries of impending insignificance.
I wallow in the wasteland of all the words
I have used and abused, sifting through sentences
for any construction that might stand the test of time.
I look for something usable to rhyme,
but reason escapes me. I stand mute before myself
in judgment, guilty of pretense and perseveration.
Talk this cheap isn't worth the air it uses, I surmise.
Time to shut up and revise.

About the Author

Mike Orlock is a retired high school teacher and coach. He enjoys travel, reading, writing, films, and spending time with his two children and five grandchildren. His short fiction has appeared in *TriQuarterly*, the literary journal of Northwestern University, and *Another Chicago Magazine*. His poetry has appeared online in "Your Daily Poem" website, in the WFOP yearly calendars, *Verse Wisconsin*, the *Los Angeles Times*, the *Blue Heron* Review, the *Peninsula Pulse*, *Moss Piglet* literary journal, and various other venues. He has published four collections of poetry: *You Can Get Here from There: Poems of Door County & Other Places; Poetry Apocalypse & Selected Verse; Mr. President! Poetry, Polemics & Fan Mail from Inside the Divide,* and *Con(Verse)sations with Myself.* His work has been awarded by the Illinois Arts Council, the Wisconsin Writers Association, and the Wisconsin Fellowship of Poets. In 2021, he was named the seventh Poet Laureate of Door County, Wisconsin.